EVERY ROUND
AND OTHER POEMS

Every Round
and Other Poems

By
Samuel Allen

Lotus Press
Detroit
1987

Copyright © 1987 By Samuel Allen

First Edition
All Rights Reserved

International Standard Book Number: 0-916418-65-0
Library of Congress Catalog Card Number 87-80159
Manufactured in the United States of America

Some of these poems have appeared previously in *Présence Africaine, Black Orpheus, Benin Review, Black World, Negro Digest, First World, American Literary Review, Nimrod, Imagine,* and *Fiction, Literature and the Arts Review.* Permission to reprint them is gratefully acknowledged. The same or other versions of some of the poems have also appeared in *Elfenbeinzähne, Ivory Tusks and Other Poems,* and *Paul Vesey's Ledger.*

Lotus Press, Inc.
Post Office Box 21607
Detroit, Michigan 48221

*In loving memory
of
Mom and Dad*

Foreword

I want to pay tribute to the vision and the courage of Naomi Long Madgett in the founding of Lotus Press and to her sacrifice and perseverance in sustaining it. Her achievement is in the tradition of Harriet Tubman and of Richard Allen who both acted on the principle of the need to take charge of one's own destiny. It speaks in the language of Langston Hughes who over a generation ago wrote of the theatre that "someday somebody will put on plays about me. I reckon it'll be me myself. Yes it'll be me." She has responded wonderfully to the challenge of that implied mandate and, in Lotus Press, has raised it to another art form.

I would like to express my thanks to Thadious Davis and to Ricardo Alonso for their insightful criticism in reviewing the earlier draft of the manuscript. I have benefited, also, from a fellowship from the National Endowment for the Arts and residence grants from the Helene Wurlitzer Foundation in Taos, New Mexico and the Rockefeller Foundation Study and Conference Center in Bellagio, Italy.

CONTENTS

BOOK ONE: Every Round

Prologue

Divestment 14
Out of the Womb, Crying 15
Africa to Me 16

Part I

In My Father's House 18
Down Belshazzar's Corridor 19
Nesshoué 20
Gougnon's Omen 21
His Magic Gone 22
The Agent in Him 23
In a Strange Land 24
The Apple Trees in Sussex 25
Homecoming 27
The Mules of Caesar 28
If the Stars Should Fall 29
Ivory Tusks 30

Part II

Necrophilia 32
Nat Turner or Let Him Come 33
Harriet Tubman 36
The Way Back 40
The Death of Uncle Tom 41

Part III

I Shall Always Hear 46
Slavery 47
Willie McGee 48

The Ballad of My Brother John   50
Springtime: Ghetto   51
The Staircase   52
Sing, Honey   54
A Moment, Please   55
There Are No Tears   56
Law and Order   57
I Heard the Siren Sound   58
I Saw the Executioner   60

Part IV

Or Countermand the Dreamer   62
Up Against the Wall   63
Sic Transit   64
The Dog Stalks Forth   65
The Lingering Doubt   66
Union Springs, Alabama   67
Summertime   69
The Invaders   70
Benin Bronze   73
Jason Stands Who Was Rent   74

BOOK TWO: *Other Poems*

Part V

About Poetry and South Africa   78
Conquistador   79
Manifest Destiny   81
John Henry   83
To Ethel Rosenberg   84
The Unknown Soldier   86
Judgment for the People   87

Part VI

This Broken Beat Imprints   90
Love Song   91
Eve   92
It Was a Lovely Year   94
The Bride   95
Antebellum   96
The Importance of Finding Ernest   97
Song   98

Part VII

The Old, Old Fakir   100
The Mugging   101
Lugano   102
And Time's Long Fire   103
Flat Tire on a Country Road at Four in the Morning   104
Spangled Ivy   105
Would Harold Somewhere Hear?   106
What Bright Pushbotton?   108

Part VIII

Definitions   110
The Lawyer   111
The Teacher and the Scholar   112
The Kingmaker   113
The President Lusts   116
The New Rules   119
To Satch   121
Touchdown   122
View from the Corner   124
State Fair   125
Small Fry Sonnet   127
In the Temple   128

Landlord/Tenant   131
Big Daddy   132
Telephone Converstaion   133
I Say, Mr. A   134
Revolt Against the Revolting   135

Part IX

Pilgrim   138
Return   139
Adumbration   140
Riverside   141
The Eternal Wheel   144
A Higher Summons   145
Cavalcade   146
Eyes Watch the Stars   147

Epilogue

Pegasus   150
The Death of Catullus   153
Invocation   156
When I Die   157
I Have Heard of a City   158

BOOK ONE:
Every Round

Ev'ry round goes higher 'n higher . . . .

Prologue

Divestment

If I could know who held the cold iron there
and branded her in blood
and singed her hair
I could tell better where my father's shadow roams
I could tell better where it roams.

If I could know where bird beaked span
    stretched huge from stone to monolithic stone
where died my mother's horrid thought in fright
    upon the lumbering mountainside
I could know better where the sheath should drop
    to spring the shimmering steel.

If I could tell in what dark sack, buffeted and tight
they locked my hope, my flawless once sane love
    and my delight
with monkey and convulsive snake, dogmatic cock
and what pale reason shrouds my soul
I could then know tonight
I could know what my need must know to feel.

Out of the Womb, Crying

And so I have come back where time its course began
I have returned to sit beneath its vine
In this same lot I first stretched my limbs and ran
In this same lot, my brother's hurt—and mine.
I no more see the shadows seeping from the sun
Nor hear the children's voices on the quiet air
For time is one again, and I am one
With all that ever was, and all that was is fair.
Days that came as filing horsemen all have fled
Into the past, the shriven and the silent slain,
But now like restless ghosts, they return where they have bled,
Stiff cerements unwinding the bright April, and the rain.

And so I have come back where phantoms play
And from the past the silent guardians stand
But there is something yet within that frets,
    it will not stay,
It cries into the night for its lost alien land.

Africa to Me

In the pit of their presumption
Encumbered yet with the weight of fear
Torn under the heel of a false doctrine
Divided by a falsely speaking seer,
We are halted at this juncture
And consider in which direction
Not to aspire.
We are weary with illusions and the years that drag,
The haste to be about another's business,
Unfurl an ever alien flag.

    I listen for the clear song
    of your sweet voice,
    O matchless one,
    who will sing an old song
    and tell in a far country
    of the foothills of an unremembered home.

They say we have forgotten;
That we parted, and forever, at the shore
In the shadow of the ships attending,
Flickering still the flame and death, the branding,
Amid the cries of terror which long years ago they bore;
That you are any curious climate
A place we're called upon to study
To be literate
    to know
Along with Peking, Angkor
    strange Tibet
    exotic Singapore . . .

Only that, and nothing more?
A curious spot, pinned on a map,
That, and nothing more?

I

In My Father's House

In my father's house when dusk had fallen
I was alone on the dim first floor
I knew there was someone a power intent
On forcing the outer door

                How shall I explain—

I bolted it securely
And was locking the inner when
Somehow I was constrained to turn
To see it silently open again

Transfixed before the panther night
My heart gave one tremendous bound
Paralyzed, my feet refused
The intervening ground

                —but how shall I say—

I was in the house and dusk had fallen
I was alone on the earthen floor
I *knew* there was a power
Lurking beyond the door

I had bolted the outside—surely
And was closing the inner when
I noticed the first had swung open again
My heart bounded I knew it would be upon me I rushed to the door
It came upon me out of the night and I rushed to the yard
If I could throw the ball the stone the spear in my hand
Against the wall my father would be warned but now
Their hands had fallen on me and they had taken me and I tried
To cry out but O I could not cry out and the cold gray waves
Came over me O stifling me and drowning me . . .

Down Belshazzar's Corridor

In the frozen silhouette of time
again the last running steps
down Belshazzar's corridor
the vacant hall of the lost gaunt men,

O father to be trod
in that land, that desolate city!
Frost of your sweat in the north!
Damnation to the south!
A legend your ancient command
The stool, wax coated
Your power a sightless mask
    nailed to the prow
      for cold, distant shores!

Strung from the mast on the fourth day
rolled above the deep
heaved from your screams into the jaws of eternal silence
O father who was torn stricken flayed
your shattered visage bleeds
    down Belshazzar's corridor
where the echoing feet and the gaunt men
    shall forever reside.

In the tale of dying embers
    is your heart's beat
In the cooling ash of ceremony
    the stuttered sparks of glory
      in the spent heat.

Nesshoué

This day I acknowledge Nesshoué
    as the goddess of the river.
Her shrine will be rich with palm oil
And her legba shall I crown with plumes.
She is the handmaiden of Maou
And will intercede for us in the day of drought.
She will ward off the evil spirits
And famine will not come to this land.
In battle will she lead us
    and she will be stronger
    and more cunning
    than the magic of the enemy.
His warriors will fall into our hands.
These things do I pray in the name of the great Maou
    and his handmaiden, Nesshoué,
    who dances by the river.

Gougnon's Omen

Shrouded voices . . .
Sea drowned silence . . .
Rising again from the green waste waters . . .
From the dispersion . . .
On wave . . . the wave . . .
The flame shadowed flight . . .
Bound flesh taught to kneel . . .
The red iron sings, promising tomorrow
Branded, they are blindfolded
Footsteps groping for the plank!
Drums . . .
The drums are sounding . . .
                    —wave on wave on wave—
Of death…a death ship and a crossing …

I see no more.
Green waters swirl across the beachhead,
Mute ceremony
    before a broken totem.
They drown the cries
    that echo
        in the darkening night.

Gougnon: an African priest known for his prophetic powers

His Magic Gone

Agassou, they cried
Has he not seen the famine
Does he not know the murder that stalks this land?
The forest is red in the night
Red with the blood of our priests
Red with the fires of the marauders
and tears stream down
    across this land.
The great Maou has frowned, and hides his face
    Lissa, his handmaiden, is silent.
She turns from the death that moves into this dominion.
Agassou sees
But snarls in his frustration
His magic gone
His power a tottering throne.

In this hierology, Maou is the supreme divinity, Agassou a lesser but powerful god whose embodiment is the tiger.

The Agent in Him

How strange again to see him—not the agent but great Glele

the sounds return

ba himba lumba mumba

once more I hear the voices

ba himba lumba mumba

The chief—huge, black
driving his men to fury.
I heard the swift voice moving across the land.

I knew in a moment his lambent will to power
would flame against the chief:
the agent in him measured Glele
by his unfond regard,
wary, till in the hush of his embrace
the agent tricked forever his arms into a casement
and broke him down, great Glele, upon his own ground.

But the tribesmen say:
"There is no chief. Cunning, unwise
he clings to power."

In a Strange Land

He sweltered in the arctic night,
forgotten the Pendergast and the hale school boys assembled.

The alabaster city gleams against the night,
and I am far from home.
Taut the bow and its slipping
in the ageless notch where I sheltered my life's core.
Strident, stringent, attending, held to the ceaseless currying,
    fitfully, faltering,
of the draining whole life's core.

Incessant the futile offensive, the untimely sallying,
toward the featureless, bloodless marauder
the barbaric Achaians, the brute Aegeans, athwart the approaches,
    stalwart, on the farther shore. Is he then dead,

the red blood fled forever
    from those heroic veins?
And Ilium's pride, thrice driven round the walls!
Apollo mute!

The eyes fell in the hushed and dying city
in tearless pity and in quiet horror,
prevision here of doom before the anguished and disjointed;
weep weep old Priam, weep, hope of your age, your heir dishonored
    dying
the city fallen
and Hecuba is inconsolable in a strange land.

    Ilium: the ancient city, Troy, of the epic Greek-Trojan war.

The Apple Trees in Sussex

    I did not climb the apple trees in Sussex
    or wait upon the queen in London town
    they courted me in sweltering Mississippi
    with birch and thong to bring the cotton down

For I have come
not to bring peace
but your heads in a block, my lovelies,
cried the captain
    of the slaver, standing
    out of Liverpool, plying
    between Guinea
    and the land of the glorious free
    the abiding place of the sullen, querulous slave;
and Montaigne reminds us that stout and aging ladies,
abandoned but not long forlorn,
plucked the eyes of their young male chattel
to shepherd a crouched submission
into their care.

Locked in the prison of those gutted years, doomed in time
pinned in the silent back rooms of unhindered desire,
to each his stock of dark rolling pride,
no seer to serve as overseer, who served as his own breeder
fertilizing the stunned flesh feeding the rows of cotton
deep in the blistering hell of Mississippi;
by the Delta they descended down
    into the pit

forsaken by Shango and Damballah, down
    to the fist and the terror, down
    to the whip and the whim
    to the blazing heat of the field by day
    and the raging lust of the big house by night and all pale
        and ravenous things.

            I did not climb the apple trees in Sussex
            I'll never hail the Queen in London town
            I spent eternity in Mississippi
            whose grace was death
                to bring the cotton down.

Homecoming

Each time that he returned to England
where he had never been
with his saxon name
and mists of english memories
and his dark blood
and his dubious blood
black and lewis carroll white
he never ceased to be amazed
at the enormity
    of these four hundred years.

The Mules of Caesar

Heavily downed with their dead the procession stopped
They regarded again the great black face
glistening ebony against the span of sand
impassive, immobile.

It does not speak!
Speak, idol!
Black sphinx, speak out!
    (... an don't say nuthin ...)
Doesn't it know I can have it whipped
into a grinning senseless chatter?
    (... Poppa always say bow down bow *down*
      when the caravan pass ...
      an don't say nuthin ....)
What what! Black wretch speak out!
    (... Poppa live a long time look like forever
      till a police broke his back with a chain)

The light beat down on the wooden black face
huge, mute, radiant in the sun.
The whips rose lazily far down the line
    and spat—
The mules of Caesar screamed
the rough flanks trembled in shame
the caravan trailed on with its dead.

If the Stars Should Fall

Again the day
The low bleak day of the stricken years
And now the years.

The huge slow grief drives on
And I wonder why
And I grow cold
And care less
And less and less I care.

If the stars should fall,
I grant them privilege;
Or should they rise to brighter flame
The mighty Dog, the buckled Orion
To excellent purposes should gain—
I would renew their privilege
To fall.

It is all to me the same
The same to me
I say the great gods, all of them, all
    —cold, pitiless—
Let them fall down
Let them buckle and drop.

Ivory Tusks

Pale and uncertain
faint in the distance
again, the shifting mists reveal
    the ivory tusks they do not want.
The bleached sands sweep my eyelids,
    heavy with revolving doors.
I turn and, reeling, turn again
but am not comforted.

I look for omen in the circling fangs
I drink huge vats of blood
I level bridges, smokestacks, monasteries
I devour houses gleaming in the sun
twining green with vine
. . . . . and yet . .

Inconsolable inconsolable
all that matters lost
ice ages of days
and I will not be comforted.

II

Necrophilia

Boring inward upon a curve
Winds treacherously
Becomes involved
Death's shadow throws the balance to the right,
    off the main course.
Success must be vicarious
Progress would be disaster
    save where an unctuous use of mass is indicated.
They here insist upon a headcount—
Although they do not lead, it's ours to follow,
    they suppose.

The boring worm fails a complete triumph
Though, since time, he has captured the pessimist imagination.
But until he has massed against the clouds
Until he has risen from his prostrate patience
We shall forever crush him
In night and down the blaze of day
We shall discover his inmost proposition
Wherever we shall find him
Though others cry
"All hail the boring worm!"

Nat Turner
or
Let Him Come

An Invitational Appeal

From the obscurity of the past, we saw
the dark now flaming face of a giant Nathaniel
calling
whosoever will
let him come.

For a moment, Turner's features softened
    he mourned the lost years
    the centuries of lined and somber faces
    the broken ranks of his people
    thousands by the tens of thousands
    torn from the soil of their fathers
    to death in life
        on bleak, distant shores.

And his face hardened
and we heard, again, the voice, calling
Whosoever will
Let him come
Let him come now
Him who can hear
Whosoever will—Come
Him who thirsts—Ha
Would drink of the waters—Come
Would drink of the waters of life
Would drink freely.

    Is there one?
    Is there anyone?

I who speak according to prophecy
In his name I say Come
For the thousands gone, Come
For the living the dead and the not yet born, I say Come

    Is there one?
    Is there anyone?
    Even so. Thank God. Praise him.
    I say Come.

    Is there another? Is there one?
    I say Come.

I which testify these things—Ha!
Surely now—who would—Ha!
Let him come. Let him come quickly—Ha!

    Even so. Thanks be to God. Yes, another!
    You will drink, my brother, of the breaking waters
    of free*dom*. Thanks be to the father!
    Is there another? Is there another? Let him come.
    Yes, come weeping. Come rejoicing!
    My God, come! I say, Come!

Yes, another and another.
Thanks be to the father.
All, come. I say, Come!

Who would drink—Ha!
Anyman—Ha!
Whosoever—

    Yes, even so. Thank God. Let them come!

Yesssss, my brothers!
everyman, anyman—in the sound of my voice!
The time is coming
Now so I testify
I which — Ha! say anyman—Ha!
which—shall drink
of the cooling waters
though he die—yessss—shall he live

    Let him come
    The sign is come
     NOW!
    Let him comoan
    Come!

Harriet Tubman
aka Moses

High in the darkening heavens
    the wind swift, the storm massing
the giant arrow rose, a crackling arch, a sign
    above the fleeing band of people,
toy figures in the canebrake
    below.

Far in the distance, moving quickly,
came the patterrollers
bloodhounds loping, silent.

Minutes before, one of the fleeing band had fallen,
the others for a moment waited
but he did not rise.
A small dark woman stood above him.
His words were slow to come and more a groan:

    Can't make it, just can't make it
    You all go head without me.

Moses pulled out her revolver and she quietly said:

    Move or die.

    You ain't stoppin now
    You *can't* stop now
    You gonna move
    move or die.

    If you won't go on
    Gonna risk us all—
    Ahma send your soul to glory, I said move!

　　　　　Long time now, I got it figgered out
　　　　　Ev'ry child a God got a double right, death
　　　　　or liberty, Move, now
　　　　　or you will die.

Listen to me

Way back yonder
　　down in bondage
　　　　on my knee
Th' moment that He gave his promise—
I was free
　　　　　　　　　　　　　　　(Walk, children)

He said that when destruction rages
He *is* a rock—
　　the Rock of Ages
Declared that when the tempest ride
He just come mosey
　　straight—
　　to my side.
　　　　　　　　　　　　　　(Don't you get weary)

Promised me the desprit hour
be the signal for His power
Hounddogs closin on the track

　　　　Sunlight

and the thunderclap!
　　　　　　　　　　　　　　(How you get weary!)

Bloodhounds quickenin on the scent
Over my head, yesss
   the heavens rent!

O He's a father He *is* a mother
A sister He will
   be your brother
Supplies the harvest, He raises up the grain
O don't you feel—it's fallin now
   the blessed rain.

Don't make no diffunce if you weary
Don't mean a hoot owl if you scared
He was with us in the six troubles
He won't desert you in the seventh.

Get on up now

That's it, no need a gettin weary
There is a glory there!

    There be a great rejoicin
       no more sorrow
       shout 'n *nev*vuh tire
       a great camp meetin
          in that land.

By fire in heaven she was guided
saved by stream
    and by water reed
By her terrible grimace of faith
    beautiful and defiant,
Till, for a moment
    in the long journey
    came the first faint glimpse
    of the stars   the everlasting stars   shining clear
    over the free
            cold
                  land.

The Way Back

I, too, see the storm coming.
Did I not guide Sherman's troops through the north of Georgia
stand firm at Shiloh
with the Rock at Chickamauga?

I see dark hands like violets like somber rhododendrons
huge tropical leaves trembling between the pole pulls
    of allegiance.

The Death of Uncle Tom

In the darkness lighted here and eerily there
    among the magnolias
The warning fled through the terrible night
Out of town! Out of town!
Flee! Run! Fly! For your life!
Your life your life!
Fly fly for your life!
On the ancient moss the serpents circled viperous
    from their mounds
For your life
Fly Fly Fly for your life!
Through the huge heavy leafed bayous
    For your life your life!
Through the canefield
The crib of his victimization
Through the cottonfield the white balls bobbing jagged
    under the ribald rising moon
Past the pit, at the edge of town, of his own misapprehension
On, on, greater than threat
      greater than fear
      greater than pain
Mounting to horror and its ineradicable dread
The obscene whisper warning shout rode down the terrible night.

    I have come back
    I have come back to this disaster
    Let my pride drink deep in the dark roaring blood
        of that castration
    The fear of the knife the dread of the rope
        the terror of the hissing faggot
    Drink deep O deep of the lost drained blood of my father
        bled in this disaster

Through the night the warning sped
And behind
they came
Swift
Sure
Deadly
Through the white fields of cotton
>	*Back, son!*
>	*Back to fear!*
>	*Back to terror!*
>	*Back to flight!*

The bolls bobbing the faces white in pursuit
I saw the sheriff's face high among the trees
    riding the vengeful night
>	*Go on back, son!*

I saw his companion
The big sloping shoulders, the huge pistols, holsters at their belts
Fools! Fools! they cried, that he should flee.

They decended for a moment to plan the chase,
    settling at an open fireplace near a cluster of tall green lichened
                    trees.
At once gray haired and faithful Tom sloped forth
    with a prudent black companion
    leashhound of his people,
    ready to be of service.

They circled around as their white masters talked
Until—a fatal accident—Tom's watch fell from his pocket
   and dropped with a declaratory clap near the pursuers.

Tom reached at once to retrieve it
But as he streched his arm, the voice came hard, deliberate,
                      commanding,
  O no you don't, worthless black son of Ham
    Hand it over! Easy, boy! You're going to give me that watch!
As though on signal, all the famed ruse and guile of Tom went
                      into play.
The two began a grotesque march around the white men,
    bending in a two-man row
    stooping low
    grinning, and around they go
    around the kettle stiff and slow
    before the masters with a bow
    to scuttle away in a keening breakdown laughter
        slapping their knees as they took off among the trees.

But then I heard him,
The watch, Tom cried, it is mine!
They had not noticed his return.
Keep back, Tom, the sheriff called.
The watch I say, it is mine, Tom fairly shouted, advancing on the
                      sheriff.
Back, black boy! Back! Have you gone mad?
The tall, muscular black, leashhound of his people, stepped
                      between.

I say, Master, Look, there is no cause for worry.
And he flashed a huge roll of dollar bills.
But Tom was on the red coaled grill, speaking with rage and fury
Accusing, castigating, never noticing the flame.
Tom's dark face dropped great beads of sweat
His short fat fist beat on the grill
His words tumbling out in a ferocity of accusation.
The tall prudent black sat silently watching by.
The sheriff warily said not a word, and walked away.
Tom followed.
From a distance, I could see him seize a rifle, aim, fire—once,
    twice, three and four times, bucking as the heavy gun recoiled.
The sheriff fell, he groaned, seized his knife
   and with his waning strength,
     rose in pursuit of Tom.
The moments passed in silence before the two returned,
    each in his death agony, the sheriff protesting,
         Why? Why did you do it?
         I heard about this in the war,
         but we get along fine down here.
And Tom, dying, sobbing,
      I put a stop to it
      At last I put a stop to it
      Maybe somebody will keep it up.
And he came to me and placed his head, the blood fast draining,
    on my shoulder.
Alarmed, I cried out, What are you to me?
But then I held him, and I comforted him
Until with a groan
He gave up the spirit.

III

I Shall Always Hear

Rebellion the outcry the flight
I shall always hear that mob still running after
the far silver call of the bloodhound
the nearing breaking through the underbrush.

My reveries shall be of thick necked countrymen
raging to the kill
their muscles massive for a bit of murder.

Their steps are here
I see the hobnailed hooves
that tread the ground, fitfully to mill around
till sharply one espies
    by brown soon reddened soil
        my flesh
the icy hands crash down
and I am driven from me.

Their sacrificial rites begin
they have anointed him
but first the gouging knife to prune the fingers
eyes, the tongue
the twitching mass is ready for the last flowing expiation
and so it is done,
the cooling flames are welcome now
the tongueless shriek is higher than the flames can writhe
into death's numbing kingdom.

Slavery
(A semi-found poem)

   Post-bellum

What was slavery like, Mamma?
   asked the daughter.

The mother turned her back
and with one quick motion raised her blouse
to reveal a thick, dark crust of scars.

That's slavery,
   she said.

What was slavery like, Poppa?
   asked the son.

Slavery was when the master told you to send Mary
up to the Big House Sat'day night,
and it didn't matter if Mary was a cow,
a horse, a pig or your wife,
you sent her!

That's slavery,
   he said.

Willie McGee

I was, I say, delighted with the splendid death row
Straight, boy, gleaming, pretty in the sun.

Because I mocked ole Willie down the last mile
howled down his wretched hymn
jabbered at his prayer,
Almighty God, I say, the Almighty God, son
    conferred on me
    the combination to the kingdom
A worthy God
    who scorns the knives of darkies pleadin.

Come along, now, Willie
You can make it
Only try.
You mustn't, I say, son
    you mustn't keep God waiting
    (with a twinkle in my eye)
Come right in
    take off your little ole robe
    no, please,
    you sit down.

The boy screamed
    frothing at the mouth
    in a spastic frenzy
    till it got downright disagreeable
So I pushed him.

When, at last
    we got that dusky brother dead
Great God Almighty said,
    I say, son
    That was mighty fine!

In the mid-fifties, Willie McGee was executed in Mississippi for an alleged rape which he and many supporting protesters contended did not occur. Outside the prison, at the signal of his death, a waiting crowd sent up a rebel cheer.

The Ballad of My Brother John

My brother John when he was trapped was wrong
to ridicule my grief and fear in song
He could not would not risk that blood was strong
but mocked my fears where in the aisle I stood.

My brother John had little use for good
He'd ground each straying seraphim he could
He'd laugh and dance and toast my
    sainted maidenhood
The fleeing years would never yield his name.

My brother John was not always the same
Be meek and mild with Jesus was his game
He'd turn the cheek and sigh, O *I'm* to blame
This did not seem to last for very long.

The sun that day came riding bright and strong
    so bright and strong
They took him out against the breaking dawn
    the wildly breaking dawn
They bound his hands and made him dance upon
                the
                  air!
I *shall* not weep
My brother
            John!

Springtime: Ghetto

Two pairs of eyes peered face to face
    in the moon's soft light.
The Ides had passed; again the Spring had come
The lucent shaft impaled the window pane
Etching dimly the quiet room
    in the moon's soft light.

Outside, beyond, the April winds
Pillaged the frail clouds,
    slashing them about
Stirred the window boxes
Cooled the night grasses
As lovers molded one another
    in the softening light.

Inside the shadowed tenement
One pair of eyes looked up,
The looming rodent's down
    into the crib
        in the moon's soft light.

The Staircase

For Bigger

> *"Abide with me*
> *Fast falls the eventide*
> *The darkness deepens"*

The staircase mounts to his eternity—
the rotted floor, the dripping faucet
all now abide with him;
the cracked ceiling, the rusted bed
    in his dark squalid chamber
abide with him now
    in the hour that is upon him.

The balance is tenuous
as his twin comes running after
the infant he let, unprotected, go
the hail of steel
stopped for a moment
lurks in the shadows.

The staircase turns
and, panting, turns—
the completely vile woman assails him
throwing livid screams from her den
far up the dark filthy hallway
until she hears the twin come running running after
    and falls sobbing and senseless to her knees.

A solitary form,
    trapped, at bay,
ruptured the glacial sky
Come, Death
Come
Take me away from here . . .!

The hail of steel began . . .
Hail cried "Hail"!

Sing, Honey

*In memory of Jessie Mae
who cleaned surburban homes*

In the distance I could hear her singing
I could see each lingering footstep
   trailing one
      upon
         another
As she trudged slowly
   toward the bus stop.

Sing, baby
Build those limpid tones all round about
Talk, honey
I understand
Talk your heart out.

Sing now, honey
Go on, baby doll
Tell em what it's all about
When they bother you again
Treat you like the vilest sin
Just you tell me all about it
And we'll straighten all those people out.

When the work is bone-ache hard
And the day drags on
               and
                  on

And night is short
   to get your slumber out

Sing, Honey
   —it is so sweet   the sound—
Sing your *heart* out.

A Moment, Please

WHEN I GAZE AT THE SUN
                I walked to the subway booth
                for change for a dime.
AND KNOW THAT THIS GREAT EARTH
                Two adolescent girls stood there
                alive with eagerness to know
IS BUT A FRAGMENT FROM IT THROWN
                all in their new found world
                there was for them to know.
IN HEAT AND FLAME A BILLION YEARS AGO
                They looked at me and brightly asked
                "Are you Arabian?"
THAT THEN THIS WORLD WAS LIFELESS
                I smiled and cautiously
                —for one grows cautious—
                shook my head.
AS, A BILLION HENCE,
                "Egyptian?"
IT SHALL AGAIN BE,
                Again I smiled and shook my head
                and walked away.
WHAT MOMENT IS IT THAT I AM BETRAYED,
                I've gone but seven paces now
OPPRESSED, CAST DOWN,
                and from behind comes swift the sneer
OR WARM WITH LOVE OR TRIUMPH?
                "Or Nigger?"

                A moment, please
WHAT IS IT THAT TO FURY I AM ROUSED?
                for still it takes a moment,
WHAT MEANING FOR ME
                now
IN THIS HOMELESS CLAN
                I'll turn
THE DUPE OF SPACE
                and smile
THE TOY OF TIME?
                and nod my head.

There Are No Tears

Consider the skyscraper
Calmly she stands
Towering above
    your cries for the ancient moorings.

Regard the impervious steel
    the assured hulk
    her feet firm
    fixed
        in the dark earth.

Not hers the insidious doubt
Not hers the utter cry
    for the lost old gods
Nor frenetic night of pursuit
    of the bright new idols.

She is.

Huge gray monolith, she stands
Massive in repose
    against the boreal sky
Indifferent even to the slow
    mole of time
    boring its campaign of attrition.

Tall and cold she stands
A stranger to regret.

There are no tears.

Law and Order

Are they safe?
Safe, are they safe?
An understandable concern.

*Black tie or turtleneck
slacks or evening gown
east side, west side
suburb, all around
are the women safe?
are the children safe?*

In the dungeons of Goreé
    This sale will be carried out
are the children safe,
    in a lawful manner—
in the ship's hold
    Order!
on the auction block
    We must have order!
are the women safe?
    cried the auctioneer.
From the sheeted Klan
    What do I hear?
from the bellied sheriff
    Going
were they safe?
    the gentleman in the black tie!
are they
    Gone!
Safe?

Are they safe?

I Heard the Siren Sound

I was in a high place
high on the quiet third floor
where I had gone to be alone
   to store my poems.
And yet I did not relish being there alone
as I watched my mother, with my younger brother
   prepare to go
she to fight the bane upon us
he to take and bring her back.
It would be late when she came back
and not too safe alone
if she came back alone
beneath the fire and stone of the fair hoodlums.

They left
I worked
   and dozed
     and stored my poems
and came downstairs
to find the widow from the house next door
watching me intently.

She said to me,
Your poems, my child,
are lying here unbound.
Hurry! Hurry! Pick them up
   before the others come,
   she fervently intoned,

They will be found
and they will burn
I know;
She smiled, her dark face twisted fiercely in a smile
I see them sifted in the blood
They will be swallowed in the dark flood
I hear the sound I see the flashing red, she said
I know and I rejoice.
Again the wizened features smiled
    and wept, she fiercely smiled
They will be found
. . . they will be found . . .

I Saw the Executioner

I saw the executioner,
    ponderous, bloated
    but—curious—he was trembling,
    could he have been repentant?

    Ah yes . . . clean shaven,
                    check!
his belly full,
        yes, check!
knees buckled
arms strapped
soul shriven
hands clenched,
           yes, check!
legs bound
eyes wild
neck bulging,
       check!
now see him

        —LUNGE—

And at his sucking after gasp, I saw
A countless host issue from that form,
Satisfied—check now!—satisfied at last.

In the big house of history, I saw
Him too stretched out, dead, done,
Cold on the slab of judgment,
Felled bv his own cold horror,
His glazed, unbelieving despair.
In his own barbaric rite, the blood cried out
His guilt; and he too, doomed,
Was seized at dawn
And driven into that quickening river
Red from the mangled host he sent before.

## IV

Or Countermand the Dreamer

It was a splendid dream, cracked
    by a rude technology
It was a glorious dream
    bushwhacked by reality.
"We shall overcome," our voices bravely sang
but we have yet to overcome
    an aircooled engine with a gospel song,
    an anti-anti missile with a fat back pot of soul;
but yet, somehow, the time, he said, would come,
    this problem would be solved,
    dream merge with matter,
    and all flesh would see it together,
a dream tricked out in peaceful discourse and compassion
in the love we dare to bear one for the other,
a dream conjured in beaten sword and ploughshare
beyond the farthest range,
    his own prodigious mountainside,
    the fruited plain,
where neither dumdum shell
    or silencer
can lay waste the dream
or countermand the dreamer.

Up Against the Wall

Have you made the scene
    in the dark
By the rock
    through the swift, raucous night
Until the holy flesh revulsed
    and the mother blew his cool?

Sic Transit

On the sloped glade
the figurines
silhouetted
in the early rays of sun
that streamed
    across the sylvan summer court
    of Louis Quinze,
a few elegantly clothed
    in satin and brocaded lace,
most shed of clothing,
the scene fixed in quiet bachanal.

We stood looking on
then drew away slightly,
turning from the patio
into the silver latticed chamber,
her gaze rising softly into mine,
but before we could embrace
I was raised to the ledge of a higher place
where, over the edge, they dropped the patients down—
a jarring slam,
and I paced a huge and grimy transit station
searching
        for the morning sun.

The Dog Stalks Forth

The chill blocked light broods in the marrow,
summer is gone.

The dark dank the chill rank mark the dark is spilled
    into the swift and deadly deep gorged river shall we run
stupendous dog, in glory.
Caress me, curve your naked fang within
with carrion spill the flood till winter come
numb the blood the jagged wound,
ambush correct the flesh upon entreaty frown
harassing prayer roar roar it down ride the frozen waste, love
assassin, fiend, O brute resplendent one.

In his far crypt
he rouses stiffens hears he hears
    my lost and shouting children.
Make haste O haste
the great dog stalks forth from his bristling hole
and I am caught with terror in the bleak dawn.

The Lingering Doubt

The lingering doubt,
the nagging doubt—
perhaps they are right,
the races are hierarchical,
despite the rhetoric of equality,
notwithstanding all the shouting.

But I'd suggest we wait;
the evidence is not all in,
man's hegira not yet completed.
Agreed, it may appear that a race
is genetically defective
by nature oppressive
an   excess of yang in the blood;
it is clear
wherever he has gone
chaos and destruction ensue,
the smashing of cultures,
the shrewd sequence of priest, soldier, merchant
pirate, slaver, buccaneer
butcher of world civilizations—
but before we close the ledger
and conclude his moral unfitness forever,
let us seek rather to contemplate him charitably
to view him as a man
    among his fellow men
endowed with the full potential of all men
and able to shed those traits
    which so mar his bloody history.
Let us hope
he may yet be raised
in the aspect of eternity,
in the sight of a generous God
to moral worthiness
or yet—and it can only finally be so—
raise himself.

Union Springs, Alabama

I pulled into the gas station
    stopping at the nearest pump.
He left his seated cronies
    and slowly, warily approached.
The pale gimlet eyes stared out.
Silence, a stubborn focus, an inquisition.
All movement in the cold gray irises stopped.
They stared, they fixed, paralyzed,
    but they spoke:

    Why do you live? Why do you breathe?
    Why do you infect the air?
    From what foul hole have you crawled?
    The air you poison sickens me.
    One, false doubtful move and we will gag
    your miserable throat till your black skull cracks
    your sockets pump blood and your wretched carcass
    swings from southern pine.

I rushed to refund his stare, eye on a staring eye:

    Pale, greaselined, lackwit face, proudly
    ignorant, bigot lost in a darkness foul,
    peering vacantly from eons of stupor, stupidity
    slack-jawed southern nobility, line of retarded Kallikaks,
    crew of mutton-headed murderers, enslavers, lynchers, rapists,
    dull wits not yet emerged from the dark ages—

tobacco spit on a bloody tobacco road!
Come, wretch, let us die together! Come, what, pale wretch,
one will surely die!

We stared into each other's face. A strange sound invaded his throat. the pale lips moved:

What can I do for you, sir?

The town of Union Springs is within a stone's throw of the nineteenth century plantation where my paternal grandfather lived in slavery until 1865 when he was nine years old.

Summertime

Again he had delivered them
    into the farthest reaches
        of a lovingly constructed hell
Quickly on his guard
    he viewed their world
        through slits of armor
But then forgetful—
    the mask would fall
        and then . . .

Fool!
Eternal fool!
Silently he walked into the simmering night.

A crowd had circled before a cafe window
    to watch the televised spectacular
At least this blunt, Kleig lighted ritual
    of Ali in the ring!
He slowed, approaching them
    Hit him!
But then,
    O dammit, he's fighting Frazier!

On down the sidewalk . . .
There, before him, stooped and spastic,
    grotesquely struggling into a corner store
    arms flailing out ridiculously
    that waythisawayeveryforlornwhichaway

Ha—
At least it isn't mardi gras for *every*—
At least—

Until suddenly he stepped ahead
    to push open the door.

The Invaders

I had chosen the town almost at random
eluding the clocks and schedules
whiplashes of I must today
the birchings of I should tomorrow.

A walk of exploration soon prompted memory
Unwittingly I had fixed upon the early home
    of New England's lustrous son.
In this sprawling river town of Lawrence, young Frost,
    almost a century before, had spent his early teens;
    and here, as the swift dominoes of the years came round,
    grew into manhood.

Now many years before, the town had built a fountain to his memory,
    latticed with scattered rock and underbrush and shrub,
    the chattering falls extending peacefully an invitation.
Installed at the sidewalk edges of a large tree vaulted park,
    the copsed memorial confronted bravely, across the street,
    the blunt facade of City Hall;
    there where old hands conspired the city's business
    and still aspiring hopefuls eagerly would learn
    the where to come and how to go.
Would Frost have winced, or would the canny sage, the arch conspirator,
    have smiled at this proximity?

An elevated plaque had been erected a few feet to the side,
detailing a brief description of the poet's life
and claiming the celebrated bard forever
    as the city's own.
It carried, too, a few well chosen lines from the poem
    he'd titled "Birches":

"I'd like to go by climbing a birch tree,
And climb black branches up a snow-white trunk
Toward heaven, till the tree could bear no more,
But dipped its top and set me down again.
That would be good both going and coming back.
One could do worse than be a swinger of birches."

I wondered, pausing for a moment, about his going
recalling the sole occasion I had heard him read—
his final appearance, it proved to be, in Washington.
Easily he had filled the great hall of the Library, that labyrinthine
    refuge of the scholar, forever confronting, without much hope, a
             mere
  stone's throw away, the Capitol.
A venerable, white haired figure, stalwart in his eighties,
    though only months remained, he had been generous.
Well beyond an hour, the crowded hall still silent, still transfixed,
    riveted on each trope, he paused, pulling a watch fob from his pocket,
      an ancient, truly monstrous timepiece.
Peering carefully into its mysteries, he proved his pedigree:
"Well, that's about enough," he said
and having then no more to say,
restored the watch fob to his pocket
and
without a further word
sat
down.

― ― ―

I stood for a lengthening moment before the plaque
    scarcely hearing the falling circling rivulets of water.
Did it depend upon the reading?
What could one make of the unintended reference?
What could he, what would he, have made of the changes in the town?
For many years it had not been
    the same quiet refuge
The comfortable anglo township of his past,
    like the Priscillas and John Aldens, now was memory.
People sat and strolled, as ever, scattered through the elm,
    the birches, poplars;
but these figures now were mostly brown; a few,
    much like the branches he would climb, were black.
The children of Cortes were here in force, with their own needs
    and dreams and accents strange and unfamiliar greetings.
As the red men had before them, the anglos had moved on,
    this time to Andover, Methuen, ever surer havens.
The plaque which bore the poet's name was vandalized and unrepaired,
    broken in several places, tilting awkwardly to the side.
The mindless play of youth, perhaps, at target practice,
    or yet a fury in a once quiet sylvan town
    struck with what fierce rage on what dark night?

And yet, far children's voices floated even then across the common
    above the self-same grasses,
The waters washed circling about the fountain
And still the poet's lines, though skewed, bore their uneven witness
    that branches stretch toward heaven
    to bear aloft perhaps, as time comes round, still other
    swingers of birches; and there will be promises
    to speed their going and their coming back.
"One could do worse than be a swinger of birches."

Benin Bronze

I gazed at Steppin Fetchit
    the West's poor clown
and, in the ship's hold of his eyes,
    saw the reddened torment of his father,

and his father's father
and his father's father's father
and beyond.

And beyond the do-rag
    and the slicked down hair
    the click of dice
    and Saturday night
beyond the fix of horse
    the cry of rage
    the flash of razor
and beyond,

from the shroud of a lost age
    the depths of a long night

emerged

    once again
    the calm and cloudless features
    of Benin.

Jason Stands Who Was Rent

The incorrigible tar broke silently across the surf
and there athwart the great oaken beam of the main sail
struck the benevolent mate to port
sweeping him into the depths.

Incorrigible still but strained
he feigned some amusement.

Banned to a foreign shore
he stubbornly rode the waves toward his death
curving a bow, whetting a blade
eyeing the huge gray belching.

But this, through it all, yielded magnificent return,
though fetched far afield for his rallying
laboring in stall, and faltering
whetting the blade of his approaching hour.

Jason Jason on the mast
Jason—rent, nailed on the northern cross of the rack
struck full the bellows of his pit
forged in mail, O Jason that was rent
that was rent, in the ebb tide of Jason.

Jason stand
stand—stand Jason!
On the peak of the cross of the reigning north
Jason stands who was rent.

BOOK TWO: Other Poems

V

About Poetry and South Africa

A Sequel

In 1928, Langston Hughes published in the *Crisis* an anti-poem:

*In the Johannesburg mines
there are 240,000 natives working.
What kind of poem,* he asked
*would you make out of that?
In the Johannesburg mines
there are 240,000 natives working.*

End of poem

    it seemed.

               – – –

In nineteen hundred and eighty, one half century later,
and Langston Hughes long dead,
the Sunday *Boston Globe* reported:

    South African miners average less
    than thirty five dollars a week,
    laboring in a painful crouch
    in waist high tunnels deep in the earth
    with temperatures reaching 135 degrees
    and more than 600 miners dying each year
        in rock slides.

What kind of poem would you make out of that?

                – – –

The stooped and stunted years themselves
    must wonder
how long still
    still how long
        must Langston wonder
about poetry and South Africa.

Conquistador

In the beginning was the Word

Cortes called upon Hatuey, the native Cuban leader, to abandon his traditional faith and lead his people into the Christian church, on penalty of being burned alive. Hatuey refused and Cortes carried out his promise.

Cortes demanded
that he lead his people
to life eternal in the cross
on pain of burning,
    Now,
he said;
but Hatuey
was as mute as stone.

The slow impenitent sweat, extruded beads
of a new adoration, uncounted, rolled
down his inverted brow;
his breath was harsh for water *water;*
his fount was the fire instead.

For Cortes, this at least must be confessed,
possessed
Toledo's eloquence with flesh
and the anvilled Roman word.
Eyes flickering over a tethered Hatuey,
frowned and muttering to himself, he said
    if he proves stubborn like the rabbi, grudging
    in the faith, a pagan who would spit upon the saints,
    it is his choice, *he's* made the choice,
    but I suspect he'll grant a few *te deums*
    over a very credible flame.

And his learned men advised on doctrine
propounded
    and refined
in the screams of a pagan nailed

to the spit of the fire, catechized
in the old time religion
in a brave new world
over the prompting blaze.

The blood fell slowly
back into the earth, a boy's voice
aged and querulous
trailed off upon the wind
through the curling script and the mist
of water falling
in the paling ash
through the lingering shroud of the flame.

Manifest Destiny

Out on that restive seascape,
algae crowding on the surface,
anemone submerged beneath the sea,
we pulled a rusting anchor
and launched the voyage
to bring us, in good time,
    a yeoman stock—
    no viscount crest, but resolute—
to a virgin soil, the New World
poised before the West
    and the sturdy deeds to come
    in pursuit of destiny.

The caravans unfolded
    on the great, shining plains.
Steadily we drove ahead
wielding, it's true, a nimble tongue
    —basic equipment, really,
    luring like the trail and perhaps, well,
    a bit supple—
but a worthy cause
a bold non-stop safari
    to a glorious destiny.

Bravely we pushed the pilgrimage
pioneers now to another sea,
the march of undaunted heroes
through the entire length of the Choctaw nation,

a ritual of title,
an advanced society—let's face it—
world weary perhaps, but lusty in a pinch,
gamely bearing the burden.

How proud we were of our first great leader,
truly first and the last among his fellows,
an undisputed gentleman
every inch of his fine, snuff dipped way.
But his guard was not slow to understand;
they'd ship your Westward Ho to Plymouth
if you so much as blinked when he closed his eyes
    and communed with destiny.

They say now it was genocide
Not victory, but genocide—
... depends on how you see it
but if they want, then "genocide"—*I'll* say it.
Genocide was the manifest
rule—it's clear enough—was our destiny.
O those were the honest, the good old days,
Anything necessary permitted, everything done.
The people joined in a great crusade
    in the march to—
Of course, it's true
the natives were rebellious.

John Henry

John Henry was a steel drivin man
    a drivin, steel drivin man
huge, dark, fearless
a behemoth of a man
prepared for hell or snow in August
a legend in a weary land,
crouched now, facing his usurper
    the rat a tat tat
    the rat a tat tat
      of a merciless machine
but still we heard John Henry laugh
O how he laughed
John Henry was a steel drivin man.

In the final hour
he outperformed if he would not, could not outlast
    his challenger,
but until the last
he was a steel drivin man.

        by whose grace
        do we assume what role
        rise to what call
        fall to what accident

The giant frame shuddered
    before he dropped
last hero against the metallic void
John Henry was a steel drivin man
John Henry was a steel drivin man.

To Ethel Rosenberg

> *The Rosenbergs were informed that if, up to the last moment, they would name their alleged co-conspirators, the President would stay the execution. The latter waited at the Washington, D.C. end of the special phone line set up for the occasion. Ethel Rosenberg's last gesture, rather, was to kiss and to comfort the grief stricken matron assigned to her care during her final days in Sing Sing.*

Richard said to Dwight
   I have a plan
   We will install a lifeline
   it will bind the air
   from here to Ossining.
   If, in the final second
   —let us make it plain—
   before the current runs
   she gives us names, as we require,
   we shall forbear.

When, by the charted standard time,
   the hour was at hand,
the wine globe of the temple
reddened and restored the flesh
beneath the Kleig light glare
of their fervid expectation.

The time had come.
Quickly she betrayed

    a kiss and a last comforting
before she stepped to horror
    final realization and a gasp,
the low wrung scream unravelling
as it raced and as it ran
on to the silent, calm Potomac.

— — —

To what grimace
and to what pain
you have come again
Jerusalem!

The Unknown Soldier

A semi-found poem

> *A gay veterans' organization placed a wreath in the national cemetery in Arlington, Virginia at the tomb of the unknown soldier.*

They placed a wreath at the tomb of the unknown soldier
paying tribute to those men, all
who went down to their deaths unknown
with their truest selves
unknown
rejoicing in the god who created them
and who knew them
and loved them
all.

Judgment for the People

Action was brought against the People of the State of New York
    by a female mute
conceived in the rape of a patient at Bellevue Psychiatric Hospital
    by a syphilitic idiot.
Complainant's suit was for compensation for existence.

The mother, tense with care,
had long renounced her dream:
    neoned idol, feted star.
The roaring in her ears did not adore
    was not an acclamation.
What desperate wit was there
    —was it could it be—
yielded to the witless
and she bore their child.

The issue found its momentary frame
    upon the network.
Consent, in this more licensed cause, was granted
    and the ratings rose.

Open forever open
    in that cleft place,
the child's lips parted wide
    and wider
as each curious second peered
    and idled by,
but still she made no sound
until her mother entered
when the straining, awkward lips extorted

> a prolonged and brutal cry
> echoing the walls the halls the crevices
> until the sound was deafening
and the mother, stricken dumb
> her draining limbs both riveted,
knew that for a moment she had fled that trap-door place.
It was simply that a child had recognized a parent,
> the frailer of the coupled pair.

Counsel for the People's case affirmed
the State cannot be held responsible
for existence caused by the criminal act of another
unless a wanton negligence
by the agents of the State
> is clearly found.

But the learned judges, wizened in the law
and long seasoned in disaster,
put the rulings to the facts, their robes in order
and they said,

> The commission of a crime
>   is not a factor in this case;
> an idiot lacks the requisite intent
> and thus his conduct must be viewed
>   simply as an act of God;
> but we reject complainant's suit on other
>   although kindred ground.
> Existence, in and of itself, however painful,
> is a condition for which the law affords no remedy.
>
> Judgment granted for the people.

VI

This Broken Beat Imprints

The rain relates a tale for all who hear
Its fitful piston pounding on earth's floor
But I have known the draught that neither seer
Nor hovering gray mist may grant before
Full lips are straightened with their measured pain
And eyes once light are gutted holes of grief, and mute
Of joy; so now I know for one alone the rain
May sing, and gaily sing—or the dark clouds recruit.

Fierce carnival it was, exultant, long
Baptismal of the dust's soft shuddering
Surrender; a poet on the earth whose wistful song
Conjured across the waste the marvelling Spring.
But you have gone. This broken beat imprints
Its monotone across the tenements.

Love Song

An arrow rides upon the sky—it does not pause or ask the way
it rides the quiet and evening air to burst upon its
startled prey.

Without a troop, a single dart has subjugated half a state—
with scorn that only eyes impart does she
retaliate.

Now beauty hides a vandal's face; yours stripped my tall heart
                          bare
 and hell is an entrancing place, because you're
 going there.

Eve

Long before the morning came—
—the shadowed prelude of the night—
I saw the maiden rapt in dread
I saw her quake in sudden fright

Her arms as death bones formed a cross
To shield her rounded shoulders bare
Her hair fell soft and tremulous
In the blunt, rapacious air

She haltingly stretched forth her arms
This way swiftly then the other
To twist and yield as though in vain
She fought a cruel and ghostly lover

Terror shone within her eyes
And terror stalked upon her face
No secret pleasure hovered there
Beneath the dread of that grimace

And then I saw two lidless eyes
Staring through her slumbrous hair
I saw the serpent rear its head
I saw it climbing, coiling there

A smile crept slowly on her face
And she declared her body bare
The serpent coiled about her breast
And tumbled coiling everywhere

Her fingers stroked its scaly length
And stroked its undulating head
Her yielding flesh in his embrace
Upon a subtle knowledge fed

The coiled length hung, and her flesh clung
To that embrace, and in its sinuous toils
She rhythmically moved, and was one
With him, locked in, rocked in his coils.

It Was a Lovely Year

I know there are few summers now
the blood at even tide
the hum of insects
    unseen in the drugged night air
    despite the irridescent light
    that shimmers, gleams
    soon to award the blow
    that only beauty can.

It seems then you will go
although you are silent
and you do not say,
and so I shall say, Go—
in peace, it was
a lovely year,
or half
or near.

Sometimes, my love, beyond the solstice, in the tundra of the year
when the cold rains have come
and the void crowds in beneath a bleak impenetrable sky
when there is no thing nothing no, not anywhere, no living thing
to cheer the blood, you
    and the faint
    and fragile
    image
    of your face
    will waken me again,
    your musing smile and your caress, your patient care
    and I shall hold your fleeting loveliness again
    and once more
    we shall touch.

The Bride

If I cannot have my choosing
Choicest of the choice among you
I'll not have the leavings over
I'll not suffer residue.

There are those who reach toward Heaven—
Far below, the scurrying mice—
You and your smug satisfaction
Keep your practical advice.

And I'd toss that chance for Heaven
On one turning of the wheel
You may have your leavings over
That! for all your even keel.

I am highly come and stubborn
Born to favor from my minions
'Tis your maid, not I, who curtsies
For your tea and toast opinions.

Bold she spoke and when she died
The mice, at leisure, claimed the bride.

Antebellum

She was defined by a narrow place,
corralled, pinned, hemmed in by denial,
bound as by steel link.
No beckoning frontier or bright expanding universe for her,
no push against horizons
nor widening sky, even for flight.
She was not destined to soar.
She was pinioned, bowed
    in a squat place.

From her cramped province she could merely
    peer beyond, eyes, for a time, still wide in wonder.
No lure of India to the East,
    or West, or Northwest Passage,
No race across the frozen tundra to the Pole, no true North
    or South,
What could she do
    but wait?
Or scarcely wait, for waiting must survive on expectation,
And how to yield to anything so irresponsible
    as hope
    for her release
    from her trapped time,
    from her small, arid space.

The Importance of Finding Ernest

Dialogue on a cruise to Nowhere

All she met was marrieds
Never any singles
You know—the same God awful joys
   of wedded bliss

But didn't she know any?

Any what? Any joys?

Ha Ha!

Well, you *know* she must have.

Who? Who was it?
Come on, tell me!

I shouldn't—really.

Tell me, tell me—!

Well, if you have to—Look,
I don't want to hear this again.
At the office, she gave at the office.

At the *office!*

Look, a whole year, dummy. What—
Oh dammit, what do you expect?
For gosh sakes, you're not really—! Here, take
my handkerchief. No, that's all right, just use it—it's Don's
idea of Christmas. Bastard! They *all* are bastards!
There there, come on, that's it. Well, for gosh sakes!

Song

He smoothed her vagrant hair
   and softly sang
      for his dreamer to waken

She stirred
   she softly moaned
She stretched forth her arms
   she ended the song.

VII

The Old, Old Fakir

I once would loiter on the Spring's sweet corner
where the berries ripen and the birch's daughters
swing and flounce about and swagger,
riot red and green and yellow
    from her magic palette.

But now I know Spring's madness.
I can neutralize her folly
    cage her bright temptation,
for I know now that Spring is lying,
each green leaf a gross distortion.
Blue skies, white clouds?
    All are con men.
And the sun? I know the sun—
    that old, old fakir!

I once was young, a devout believer.
I bathed in its blazing glory,
arms stretched to the rising sun.
But now the world is flat again,
    old, without an issue
there is no omen anywhere.
For I know now the Spring is lying,
for Winter came;
    the clouds, the frigid snows, the knifing winds—
    they took pains to teach me.

I was not their brightest student
but they refused to give up on me, they persisted.

Now I understand.

The Mugging

Urban Sunset

I never saw so deep a wound
    to flow without a cry
As evening's bloody razor slash
    that touches up the sky
And races on the ashen clouds
    appalled the day should die.

LUGANO

Children rouse the neighborhood on the swings in the playground in the early fall morning.

In the early

It was morning

Upon the sun

     the sun spun morning

I was ^lifted^ into glory

I could ^see^ the ^swings^ of ^heaven^

Racing ^rising^ to the swiftly

And the ^tumbling^ to descending

And the ^children shriek^~ing~ gleely as they ^split^ the Italian ~sky.~

And Time's Long Fire

The bars came over the even night
Borne in upon the cold October air,
That, too, is me . . .
Still part of me . . .
He slowly said;
Not my long buried griefs nor Paul de Vence
    nor Tasco, no
Not Port au Prince, Sienna, Munich no, nor Blida
Has yet erased it—
The smoke of autumn in the midwest skies
Brown fields where they have lain upon Ohio,
the dead and simple leaves that feed the fire;
It was two continents ago I saw this sun in its decline
The darkened silhouette of tree
And now, beyond, the low flung horseshoe of the moon
Where my youth's blood aspired
    to that refrain
The restless years have fled
but I am riveted again, once more
      by that refrain;
And when that vagrant refrain dies
Smoke—
The smoke of time—
And time's long fire
Are in my eyes.

Flat Tire on a Country Road at Four in the Morning

Gigantic . . .
Is the night . . .
The patient stars creep slowly . . .
Across the inky fold . . .
All around is peace . . .
The dove keeps his repose . . .
The brilliant dawn has yet to rouse

And doff her sullen lover . . .
The quiet stars look down . . .
The vast . . night . . sleeps on . . .

Spangled Ivy

Testament of a Contrarian

They store the grain beneath the sun
I court the apple of my eye.
They seek the fire when day is done
And I the parting melody.
They learnedly must excavate
Each musty hieroglyphic style;
I'd much prefer to cultivate
The langorous haunches of the Nile.
They would dissect the mystic night
Proclaiming where each star should lie
As I look up in dumb delight
That spangled ivy climb the sky.

So shall they harvest of the sun
And they shall burrow winter by
    And I shall rise when summer's done
    And follow a lost melody.

Would Harold Somewhere Hear?

It is a cold clear night
    a brittle cold
Without a sound to brush that veined expanse;
The stars hang sharp and clear
The moon, a displaced beacon light
Streams down upon the silent buildings
    robing them in black
    and widow's gray
    and ceremonial white.
I think of Harold who walked with me
    beneath these stars.
But Harold is dead.

I know it was four thousand miles away
A thousand years ago, I know
Lost in a Dresden raid.

And yet I wonder if, in that huge fist of space
Harold is somewhere.

The distance and the years, and yet sometimes it climbs
    and reaches through and crowds into the mind
And Harold—did *he* mind, did Harold mind too much
Is he still here to mind
The eyes wrenched wide in sharp surprise
The blood's involuntary cry
Did Harold weep against the unrelenting moment
Or did he wanly smile before he plunged
    and grasped his fate
    and died?

I wonder if I shouted loud enough
—if I should send his name a piercing scream
  against the cold black wall of heaven

Would Harold somewhere hear
And, trembling, cup his ear
And know that it is I?

What Bright Pushbutton?

A clever pushbutton, Juan Trippe,
Should your swift travelers from Montego Bay
Wish for the cabin attendant;
A "cabin"—!
    as though a gleaming galleon, riding the centuried main!

At lunch, what bright containers for the entree,
For the Roquefort, even for the Ceylon pepper;
As we dine, what vast motors reassure us
    fourfold, roaring their massive
    insistence on their proud course;
What mammoth wings to strike the wind
    in slow majesty
    raising and lowering their flaps
    indifferent to the waters far below.

All is well,
Is it not, Juan Trippe?

But this inscription to the rear?
"Salida de Emergencia" it warns—
It scarcely fits the smooth sure pace.
Is there something you have not forseen?
Or engineers could not contrive
    by blueprint and design?
But so I was wondering—

What bright pushbutton will you have, Juan Trippe
When God looks down to see your Lilliputian fleck
    against the backdrop of his heavens
And smiles
And reaches down
And brings his children home?

Juan Trippe: former president of Pan-American Airlines

VIII

Definitions

A thingumbob is an object similar to but sharply
    to be distinguished from
    its linguistic cousin, a thingamajig,
the familiar name for the first being Bob (Mr. Robert Thingum)
the other widely known for his wildly popular Saturday night Jig
    (Mr. John Thingama),
both in their deeper structure being of an entirely different order
    from a doohickey,
an enormous welt raised by a swift blow to the skull
which, again, in its indwelling and often throbbing thingism
is not to be confused with that transcendent incarnation
that other thingumbob, that epiphanous thingamajig, a
whatchamacallit,
which is, of course, an entirely different gismo,
according to the most recent and highly authoritative work
                on the subject
                by whoosis.
In these distinctions, a careful uniformity is essential.
On language as on a trapeze, agreement is all.

The Lawyer

sipped his glass and dryly said

    I confess, I'm a rented gun I am not
    Galahad I stalk the sainted buck
    in the valley of my very
        personal
        gain;

    but if they smoke me out—
    exposed, beaten off, pursued,
    when the cry goes up

his lips absconded nimbly in a smile

    look for me with you on the mountaintop
    denouncing evil invoking good
        I'll *be* there
            on the highest bluff
    battling in the People's name.

The Teacher and the Scholar

I had noticed her distinctly,
    the earnest pedagogue, before.
She was young and she was comely,
    lines like a racing schooner,
        a face to lead to folly and disaster.
A bemused, ironic fate had fixed her lot
    with this restless band of scheming ragamuffins.

Now hotly flushed, she was indignant:

"Richard Goodman," she was shouting
glaring fiercely down the hallway.
She had bolted from the classroom
but much too late to catch the small, decamping figure
which had struck and cravenly turned tail and run.

"I *mean* it!
I do *not* appreciate your kicking in my door!"

It is not at all
    that I fail to understand the teacher.
I understand the teacher fully;
I, too, have had my patience tested to the utmost.
No, it's rather that I understand the scholar more.
If I were in her class
    that's exactly what I'd study, I'd do take-home.
Frankly I would relish
    simply kicking in her door.
It's true I'm not as young or quick as Richard
but I'm convinced I'm equal to it
I confess—I'd love to do it
    just to kick smack in her door.

So I cannot honestly side with the teacher
    against Richard,
now can I?

The Kingmaker
or
Ward Boss

I tell you, boy
You've done a few things for the party.
Boys all been looking at you—
    Thanks!
We're going to have to see what we—
    Yes, thanks!
    Seems like today I'm always dropping something.
What was I say—Oh yes—Don't think we haven't seen
    the work you're doing—
    That's right—the ash tray there—fine, thanks, unnh hunh—
As I was saying, Don't think we haven't seen—we've *seen* it, boy.
Now what—what was it that you wanted? Oh yes, we're going to see
    what we can do.

You know, the people in this country—
    If you'll just push that brass spittoon a little closer—
    Fine, thanks!
Now as I was saying. No, wait a minute, son. Let's see just what we've
              got here.
No, no, we're going to find a way.

You know, old man Carruthers's
    not what he used to be.
He won't be there much longer.
Truth of it, should be gone today.
Boys don't want to crowd him—
Missus sick for years, the kids, you know.
Then, too, he listens
    to what we've got to say.

But let me see.
Now I've been thinking—
    That's it. No, that one.
    I always wear the gray. It's live enough, you know—
    —you've got to watch these things—and still it doesn't bray.
Now I had this in mind—Do what you want!
    Thanks! Good! Feels fine! Just fine!
You see, we might work something with the Second District.
Now how's that sound.
Just try that on a minute.
That's opening up.
I keep em upstairs always owing something—unwashed bastards—
    and I know just how to make em pay.

But boy, the thing that's really it,
It's not the District, it's the Commission, The *Commission,* boy.
That's what keeps the party happy, keeps *everybody* happy.
Little stink at first, of course.
Bar Committee—scream downstate!

But that won't last.
We'll have Jim ring the Gov'nor—keep em off ya.
It always dies away.
One term a that—man need not be a tar baby—
    and you are fixed for life.
And clean, boy—at least most of the way.
But they can never touch you, we'll show you how to work it.
One term a that, Son, and let me tell you,
You've really had a day.

Don't get me wrong.
The District's good—it's good for show.
But the *Commission*—that's the thing, son.
Think on it, boy.
Chew it over for a day.
Talk to Bill, we'll get him outa chambers.
Then see me first thing Sat'day.
Now don't you worry—you leave it up to me.
    No, nevermind. I've got it. Well all right. Thanks, then.
You're with us, son.
I can see you're on the way.

The President Lusts

> *In a magazine interview during his first presidential campaign, President Carter confessed to a feeling of lust at the sight of a pretty girl.*

The President is a self-confessed heterosexual
The President of the United States of America openly admits
    he lusts after women.
An amazing state of affairs—
The President is an avowed woman luster.

Responsible and decent citizens deplore this sort of thing,
The civilized instincts of all honorable men and women
    compel them to recoil from it, to shun it.
They would have no stomach for it,
and I fully endorse this position;
but, in an effort to speak straight from the shoulder,
    I will, at least, though cautiously, confess
I am an unconscionable ice cream luster
a miserable maple walnut luster
an abandoned vanilla luster, a shameless lemon luster
and, moreover, a cookie luster: a brownie, a congo, a gingersnap luster
but obviously, this doesn't begin to compare with the President.
Our President, our *President,* mind you, is a
    self
        confessed
           flesh
                luster!

Again, I insist,
    an incredible state of affairs!
Truly a national scandal. The matter has gotten completely out of hand!
You hear the children in front of the White House
    at hop scotch in the square:

        the President lusts
        the President lusts
        hotly after
            human flesh!

and the kids on 14th and U with their syncopated beat:

        ole prez lust
        ole prez lust
        he's hot hot
        —flesh flesh!

The President is, in fact, it is rumored, a leg luster,
never really a lack but surely a back luster,
also a bust luster.
A confirmed case, this we know, a definite case of bust lust
decidedly a bust luster.
You can bet your dough on that,
he *is* a luster, buster.
And not simply after one, it's clear,
    in time it would by many.
(Shades of Nero and Caligula who each

   in his insatiable turn, scared the wits
     out of the population!)
O he is a monstrous luster!

The nation should be warned!
The President of the United States is an avowed woman luster
The President is a miserable, self-confessed het er o *sex* u al
Most shameless of men
The President lusts!

The New Rules

He amused himself.
He urged her to eat well
    because he'd sleep much better;
and after coffee, Napoleon
and ripening glances,
before the waiter came, he said
    if she were kind
    and paid for both their dinners,
    he would not run or fight
her boss top dollar right
    to take advantage of him—
    think about it.

Ouuuu, she said. Ouu Ouu Ouuuuu, she said;
and she thought about it.

If I
    should choose
to use
    my mastercharge,
should I then have him like a basted boar
    securely trussed
    and plucked
    and sectioned for my exploration;
or lobster mousse, or devil's food,
or creme eclair
    with custard filling;
or like a simple snack—hot dog!
less the wrapping;

or since I've won advantage
should I then take him home and drive
    a stinging slam into his court,

my game, *your match,* my love
and send him packing, sacked
and slowly flushed and baffled;
but winning, no, is not the only thing;

Or shall I hold his head
here in my lap
    like so
as the new light comes,
and he has curled into his dream
in the quiet
afterglow,
and reach . .
and seize . .
    my razor sharp and healing scissors
    here, like so
and slip away these worn and heavy locks
one
    like so
by one
    like so
    like

    so.

To Satch

Sometimes I feel like I will *never* stop
Just go on forever
Till one fine mornin
I'm gonna reach up and grab me a handfulla stars
Swing out my long lean leg
And whip three hot strikes burnin down the heavens
And look over at God and say
How about that!

The career of Satchel Paige, the legendary baseball pitcher, extended into five decades.

Touchdown

In memory of Hymie

We played in a sidewalk bordered sandlot which we dubbed the Dump, back in Cleveland, Ohio during our teens.

What tricky thief could ever steal
from fate a moment half so fine
as when I faded
               falling
                         fifteen
                               yards
behind the line of scrimmage
   the day was clear
surveyed the embattled field
   blazing, bold the sky
stretched my heroic arm
   the hit men closing on me

and feinting four dazed, howling, scowling hoodlums silly
shot a smoking bullet
into the raw October air . . . . .

saw it rise into the sunlight breaking wide
into the daylight
   still rise and riding, rising
until it eased
               into a curve
                            at last decending

flying home now to its shadow
saw it strike the fleeing Hymie saw him turn
and trip he staggered clutched the bullet
to his sweater and collapsing on the sidewalk
held it there . . . .

— — —

How far away
And yet, as yesterday, I see them silent, all
    impaled upon the moment
    mute hieroglyphs that mark the time
    a late noon copy scripted
    on the skyline,
the outstretched arms, the angled speeding legs
a frieze of swastikas across the field
like soundless phantoms, soon enough to fade
to wander off to home and other fields and destiny
and why is your storm jacket dirty and you are late
but they alone will know how on one raw October day
Hymie ran and Hymie ran
and scored
         a
            TOUCHDOWN!

View from the Corner

Now the thing the Negro has GOT to do—
    I looked from my uncle to my dad
Yes, Nimrod, but the trouble with the NEGRO is—
    I looked from my dad to my uncle
I know, Joseph, but the FIRST thing the Negro's got to do—
    It was confusing . . .

This fellow, the Negro, I thought excitedly,
    must be in a very bad fix—
We'd all have to jump in and help
    —such trouble
    —all these things to do
I'd never HEARD of anybody with so many things to do
    —GOT to do!
I intensely disliked such things
    —go to school, wash your ears, wipe the dishes
And what the NEGRO had to do sounded worse than that!
He was certainly in a fix, this Negro, whoever he was.

    I was much concerned as I looked quickly at my uncle
Now the thing the Negro has GOT to do—!

State Fair

> *Dad took us to the annual fall*
> *State Fair, which we discovered*
> *to be "reserved" on the weekend.*

We took the road out to the Fair
To be told arriving there
That it did not run to colored
    on the weekend;
They suggested with an air
Phase your brown selves out of here
The brotherhood is over
    on the weekend.

We cavort here blond and fay
In an uncorrupted way
We are spotless like the lily
    on the weekend;
Don't insist, be nice and go
Vanilla yes—chocolate no
Now don't revert, just Go Go Go
We are out of wahta—melon
    for the weekend.

This is an *ivory* display
We mean everywhichaway
Head neck shoulders hip hurray!
You be um nice—*You* go away
We dispense with the brother
    on the weekend.

Supremely fair and debonair
They scarcely seemed to be aware

The six of us were really there
    on the weekend,
Until Dad took us by the hand
Until our *father* took command
And told us that we would not stay
And led his straggling troops away
    on the weekend.

Small Fry Sonnet

"What happened to your bike?" he shouted out
Across the field, his voice confident of
Answer, though he stood at half the height, about
The other's waist, who towering above
And walking on, cast back assurance, ". . . the bike's
All right, a kid on Twenty-Second Street
Had it," but mumbled, knowing language strikes
Most shameful depths when made merely to treat
The fancy of these half-ripe denizens
Of field and shack and each deserted flat
Along the tracks. The information wins
Profound concern, "Can you a-*maj*-un that?"
And with a face wrought fierce in tribal strictures
He whooped his way—O pioneer—to the moomcowboypichurs.

In the Temple

Were you there
 when Jesus jump down the throat of the money changers
It was somthin else
Like a maniac, never saw him such a state.
Always so peaceful, you know
Yellin, Get out! Get out!
And when they don't move fast enough, took a whup—
Did you ever!
Snatched it from somebody—didn't carry one
 —polices left it—
and that man began to swing away, I'm tellin you—
Sweet, gentle Jesus!
Meek, mild Jesus!
Somebody *else*! Not that mister!
Scowlin, racin round the temple
left arm pumpin up and down
 —never knew he was left handed!

When the people got they wits
they ran and told Mary
Mary, your boy Jesus he in the temple
goin *crazy*!
He beatin on the money changers
all up'n down the buildin
from the altar clean out the door!

Mary run as fast she could, poor Mary
she lately have such trouble with that boy
throwin off her apron as she ran
come tearin round the corner just when Jesus
was workin on a bunch like he splainin to a dusty rug

Ka-whamm, O whup say
Mary startin up the steps
hands up in the air
    Jesus, ma little Jesus!
Ka-whamm, O whup say.
Get outa here, he yell!
    Jesus, ma little Jesus
    I thought I taught you never hit nobody
    Leave that to the polices
    That's *their* business!

But that boy was outa his head!
He say,
    Look out, Mama
    Look out now;
    Get outa the way, Mama
    Mama—you gonna get *hit!*

Did you ever!
I'm tellin you—
Never in my borned days!

Mary first sorta weep'n she moan
But then she say
    Stop this foolishness at once!

But naw, nuthin for it,
    Mama, these is money changers, they's money changers, Mama
    Can't you understand *that*?

Well, that's the way it went.
Naw, she can't control that boy. Can't control him no more.
Just had to wait til it was all over, fore she could get him
  t' head back home.
I was followin from a distance, she's carryin on somthin awful,
  You forgettin your raisin 'n evathing? People gon start wondrin
  whose chile you are. Whuppin people! You wait till I tell your fatha!
  Lord knows what he's gon do to you!
I'm tellin you. And funny thing. After all that who-struck-John,
the quietest look came over that boy's face.

Landlord/Tenant

Landlord come round here other day talkin bout
he have the *unit* to fix it, y'unnerstan?
Claim he have the *unit* to fix it.
You know what it was?

Naw, man, what was it?

It was a unafied lie!

Big Daddy

They say
That at the end
The light
Growing dim
And dimmer
The pulse
Almost
Still . . .
Adam still
Big Daddy still
Was able
Always Big Daddy able
To confer a wan slow grin
When told that they were fighting
Hotly feuding
Even at the end
To the very end
To win the disposition
Of the remains . . .

Go, Big Daddy
Go, Big Daddy.

It was reported that as the end drew near, the women in the life of the legendary preacher/politician had not come to an agreement over final arrangements. He had often been referred to, both by himself and by members of his congregation as "Big Daddy."

Telephone Conversation
or
Don't Just Stand There

Now look, I'm no bigot but—
What gets me—
I saw it on Channel 7
That movie star
   Extremes, Supremes
   something or other
   raving over her German maid
              Hilda is a real find, she says
              Why Hilda is a jewel, like that
              Why hon-ey, Hilda is a jew-ul.
              She said, That girl's so neat
              and works so fast
              I don't know what I'd *do* without Hilda.
              And then got the nerve to say,
              Why I can trust Hilda with my *personal* things.
Right there on Channel 7
Exactly what she said.
Now I ask you, what in the world are we com—
Oh my chest—I feel faint—
Willa Mae! Quick!
My pills—get my pills!
Don't just stand there!

I Say, Mr. A

When
At the close of war
Louis Armstong returned to the continent
The gentlemen of the press crowded about
Inquiring,

        I say, Mr. Armstrong
        Which reception did you feel was wah-mah
        That before the wa-ah
           or this?

And Mr. Armstrong replied to the gentlemen,
Saying,

        I didn't have no thuh-moma-tah
        but they was both a bitch!

Revolt Against the Revolting

It is reported in the press there is a move afoot to oust the 82 year old Dobson Campbell as the Grand Exalted Ruler of the Benevolent Protective Order of Elks. The grounds for the proposed ouster are alleged mismanagement and senility, the latter based upon public displays of absentmindedness at many lodge affairs around the country. At a reception in Campbell's New York Hilton Hotel suite during the organization's annual convention, onlookers reportedly watched in amazement as the Grand Exalted Ruler ate grapes and spit both the skin and the seeds on the suite's expensive carpet as if this were the proper place to direct refuse.

If this is representative instance of the alleged misconduct, it becomes clear that, as some have suspected, the attempted ouster should be opposed by all right thinking men and women. It is indeed a scurrilous attempt, an effort by jealous little ant biddies to undo a great leader. It is a classic case of ambitious infants still ringingly wet behind the ears having the audacity to try to bring down a glorious old master. Examination of the conduct they cite reveals at once how distorted is their understanding.

Who is the Grand Exalted Ruler? Dobson Campbell is the Grand Exalted Ruler. Now we put the key question. Whoever heard of a Grand Exalted Ruler who must be careful where he spits? As *the* Grand Exalted Ruler—they properly have only one—he must be able to sit in the room, stand in the room or dance about the room, eating of the divine fruit, the grape, as the godly Greeks before him, and in exaltation spitting the skins and the seeds wherever he, in his grand and exalted status, pleases. Does a truly grand exalted ruler fuss about—"Pardon me, pardon me. Is there a wastebasket?" to find a receptacle, perhaps a garbage pail or an inglorious commode upon which to bestow his creations? (His critics in abysmal ignorance refer to them as "refuse"!) What a truly ignominious thought!

But in their revolt against the revolting Campbell—the allegedly revolting Campbell, we must in fairness insist—his critics in horror clamor, "But he spits *both* the skin and the seeds." How false how petty a distinction, as if one by itself would be acceptable but the two together not. How crass their comprehension, limited their understanding! It is in beautiful symbolism of his boundless love for his brothers (and the Ladies Auxiliary) that through the skin of the grape he offers his mortal self, through the seed he bestows his immortality, eternal blessing upon thousands of Elks yet unborn. It could not reasonably be expected, of course, that he forego the juice.

And then some, mind you, some—we cringe to admit it—bow their heads and sadly lament, What will *they* think of us? O shades of Thomas, Fetchit and Jemima! Don't they understand why these hotels were built? They were built precisely because we needed places across the country where we could convene and our rulers could live out the meaning of their exalted status. Conrad Hilton knew this. That is precisely why he constructed these secular temples. Messieurs Sheraton and Statler were much later in coming to this understanding and that is why we favor Mr. Hilton even down to this day.

IX

Pilgrim

Discarding the brassard of another day
The cockade of another hour
He took a new and dubious path
Whereon, at last, the midnight came
And stricken, in his thirst,
He tapped the rocked inscription where he lay.

He gazed into the huge academy of the night
The canopy of starred misdirection
The lost route of Charlemagne to the sea
The pole pull of desire
The stone way of the Saducee.
Great starry school, he said
So calm, serenely treacherous,
Teach us to block out thy sight
And not to pray.

He slumbered then, and dreamed awhile
And all the saints of history
Shall pass in frugal panoply
With enigmatic smile.
And he shall rise and deeply bow
And wait upon them as they come
The soft melodic tapestry
The frayed unfolding symphony
Of their bright martyrdom.

Around, the phantom light wherein he lies grows dim
The skies dark;
Nebo's brow
Is shrouded in the mist.

Return

Almost within the Garden
elbowed upon the wall,
his bearded voice sprang out at me
I fell, he made me fall.

And darkness shall enfold the earth
and sleep attend the langorous rite
except for him who takes his stand,
lone watchman through the tedious night;

but long before the dark shall flee
the first reconnaissance of gray
his head will nod, his eyes slowly close
and he will brood upon the day;

and he will see me in a dream
and he will reach to smooth my hair—
I'll move—and quietly look at him
standing there.

And rousing, he will long regard
his silent, dark domain
and, sighing, mutter to himself—
perhaps, at last, he would explain:

He knows my word is final, yet
it has been long, I fear;
those eyes, how dark with suffering
and I . . . I'm lonely here . . .

Adumbration

So they remain, worried lest he should impinge
upon the leafed caress autumnal penitence commends
before the first fat forty of his soul's dark adumbration.

Yet are we here under this glare
    fierce semicircle of light
    targets of the unseen
    awaiting the future in staccato.

Worried lest he should stumble and fall
and never really rise again
never again,
he shall not rise,
though glazedly he go on for some measured miles
in form or out of form,
by whose forensic fancy does it matter
. . . nor does it matter.

The audible supplication through the leaves
attends an obtuse truth,
in the sense of the difficult to bear.
It sheds it professorial robes
and approaches, whispering.

Riverside

The mist lifts measureless
    over the valley
a sumless mass of forces and event

And so am I divided
    one and ten thousand fold:
this flesh, a dream, a wish
lust and satisfaction
    trailing their regret
or solitary wreath of love, or reams, or widest oceans of
    and there, frustration
ambition and remorse, roller coaster of desire
accordion of purpose and retreat
the gulls careening dialectic, plunging
    each time to rise again
    over the shore.

A flux of shifting entities
numerous, dissonant,
I can never order them
arrange them neatly, long stems contrived
assign them attributes and functions, roles, duties
the wind rushes through
    stirring a thousand senses, blind compulsions
    rousing and dispersing
I am shaped by passion, gusts of whim, impulses
    transformed by fancy, idle thought, mere accident
random toy of vision and myopia, ideas, ideals
    their orphaned resolutions
an obligato of elation and despair as the swirl of forces

  coerces the heart assaults and distorts the brain
if there were any lasso begging order, it is slipped
if bonds, they've broken
I am as definitions of a word, many and unrelated
  chameleon with the context shrewdly taking on
  the tint, each standard spec every color of the field

One and various
diffuse and protean
  like the sand
no pattern seems to hold
neither place nor time nor sequence certain
epoch and continent, every category falls away
the blinding storm hoods me
  I am its flash and flare
the hurricane
  and the leaf buffeted before it
the filed and tabulated summers backward fade
and I am Agonistes
  staring at the booted foot
  as vision slowly drains
the upturned underbelly thrilled to grapple with the blade
I am the eager Seigneur
  and I am the peasant groom
  who waits across the moat into the dawn
a nocturne idle on a summer's night
the indifferent clock its tick and tock
deliberate
  upon the wall,
each opened hand forced to the wood
  the steel that allocates the bone
Judas restless—just one kiss
the serpent swarming on the rock
a fine Venetian hand entwined
  a blameless handkerchief

the manacled Sephardim lunging vainly from the smoke
the Huguenot persuaded after much upon the rack
the Ashanti head corrected in the wooden block
    on the quiet and sunny trail
    that winds to Christianburg

I am the meditative skull at Nagasaki
the standing doorless doorway
the ruined and the leveled wall
I am the doting mother who dances for her brood
    to violin and Brandenburg
    through the doors of Buchenwald

The mist of the morning rises still across the valley
ascending to its source
    beyond these clearing skies,
for rains again to gather
to find this valley and the streams
    that feed the river
to solve again the myriad drops
    moving down the long confederate pathway
    to the sea.

The Eternal Wheel

I swear that I care not for orchards, rich with ripe berries
I scorn the lagoon, sails exploding the sky

    I revolve upon the eternal wheel
    And shall come round—hail the Ram
    to the slow naked toll of destiny.

The pale lie of the day has never deceived me
Always I have sensed its wretched deception

    The throbbing wings of my myriad myrmidon
    Have whispered to me have talked to me
    Have brushed across my shoulders.

Yet am I torn and divided
Yet am I driven apart
For the orchards are precious, of silver and gold
For the orchards are precious, of silver and gold.

A Higher Summons

In the mirrored wall
receding before the standard bearer
came the holy vertiginous encampment.

Not because of the exacting wraith did it come
but dutiful and obedient to a higher summons did it appear.

In the temple of smoke, hovering and measured,
I learned of its coming
but put little store in it
weighted as I was by the shadows on the wall
until I was smashed by its voice
shuddering, maimed
bitten by flame
almost persuaded.

But the washed vista faded in the rolling panorama of the years,
the tall stuccoed houses lured me on,
and I went on,
attentive sometimes,
sometimes indifferent,
more than once stoned for blasphemy.

The pebble in the pellucid lake has broken the silence
    here in this encampment
I listen calmly in the still noon.

Cavalcade

*the dance of
the Sarcophagi*

We went in darkness beyond the fading light
beyond disaster and recall
we jumped holy in the night

Camp by the winding sheet
rebuff the maggots
theirs will be time

How can we deny the bright vision
of the soul's torment
struck from this shadow?

Come, Sarcophagi
upright dance
in pale light.

Shall we see Jerusalem
or blight?

In canine sorrow, pierce the last refrain

Bootblack rise before the startled flight of swallow
Come Treetops, Rolling Hillside, Dazzling Pulchritude
Candescent, Mobile Fractionless
Come Now, Jump to Sight.

Eyes Watch the Stars

*Eyes watch the stars
they are not higher than the year is high.*

Casting shadows
from the midnight
stands a caravan upon the sand.

The waters falter and turn back
cringing from swift terror in the husk.
A blanket will encompass all of them
and a world besides.

I personally look for little from this mess of star and sand,
the desert will dry beneath the red sun.

*Eyes watch the stars
. . . . the stars . . . .*

Epilogue

Pegasus

The winds strong
visibility—zero
co-pilots waiting to descend
the system calling sharply
state who you are and your position
identity must clear before each ship comes in.

In a gift shop as we waited
a wizened little woman sold mementa, assorted bric a brac,
    a strewn array of half forgotten ware.
With time to occupy, I wandered over, browsing through
    the vintage stock   she offered.

            — — —

A rustic cabin hovered high above a mountain stream
which through uncounted generations past
had worn a yawning chasm
    deep in the stubborn, rocky soil
the cabin, balancing above, a fragile bridge
    across the void.

I peered inside and entered
    upon—to my surprise—a brightly glittering floor
the room as we advanced grew large and larger
as though a festive court or great ancestral hall;
but then, at length, emerging,
    we stood upon the farther precipice
    still high above the wandering stream below.

My gaze turned back and to the side—
   silently the woman pointed—
I saw recessed a secret entrance
   when without a sound it opened, leading
   to a hidden staircase
     winding down
       and down
         down
   until at last it came
   to the floor of the ravine
   and the slowly flowing stream.

There—still peering down, she beckoned me
   still closer—
sitting motionless among the trees
were two grave and formal lovers
   in the late afternoon
where only the hermit thrush was heard
and the liquid murmur of the stream.
On brown and withered leaves that long years ago had fallen
sat the two and formal lovers
in the deep mountain forest
   in the quietly waning afternoon.

Silently we watched them
until, carelessly, my sudden move
   my arm displaced a solitary leaf
   which spiralled slowly down between them.
   Surprised, the two masks of their faces lifted . . .
   two petals in the half light . . .
   as we drew ourselves away.

―――

I said, Why it's amazing
I would certainly like to have it
but I'm sure it's too expensive
perhaps another time, I'd like to take it, but, perhaps,
    another day.

The wizened little woman smiled mysteriously
and, reaching down beneath the counter
drew forth two finely sculpted horses
and launched them high into the air
and round and round the shop they flew
until she stopped them
and wrapped them
and, bowing quaintly,
presented them to me.

At last I heard
The words at last sank through
I turned—my flight was called—
I turned again, but she was gone—
I hurried on to catch my plane.

The Death of Catullus

Catullus stood with the others, attendant
    in the court of Caesar,
the marble floor resplendent
the halls columned high in achromatic white
    and serpentined in beaten Carthage gold.
It was a quickening whir, at first scarcely heard,
as the lance, at his command, unerringly flung,
raced to its mission, reddening the marble floor.

It was Caesar's whim petulantly to explain,
    "As in the painting, simply as in the painting!"
At his finger snap, the tempera, telescoped swiftly
    back in time
    from thirteen centuries beyond
    was carried forward.
The scene, precise in detail, exact in replica—
    there in the painting, now on Caesar's floor,
    the two slain lords.

    "Look now"
the emperor suddenly exclaimed,
    "at this exquisite labor of the Medici:
its peerless coloring, superb fidelity of detail, its subtle
hum of expectancy. Let each warrior to his peril
recognize himself and find the weapon—lance, net, sword, chain—
fit to his station."

Terror seized us as we gazed
    for one frozen moment, until, as on command,
we broke from our places, surging
    into the armory, each seeking
    the instrument of his salvation.

Caesar surveyed the turmoil, lips pouting to a smile,
as we busied ourselves
rushing and shouting for arms.

At last we stood, breathless and fearful,
    each with his weapon.
The Emperor looked bemusedly about the huge, now silenced hall.
His gaze roved among us, fixing first on one and then another
    before it came ominously to rest, our heads turning
    in unison to ferret his intention.
Even as we looked, we heard the whimpering lament,
    "Catullus, ah Catullus!
    And I so fond of Catullus!
    Come, sweet! Beside me! Won't you come!"

Our eyes were riveted upon him as with slow, reluctant steps
Catullus advanced, mounting finally the dais.

Concern was playful impulse on the Emperor's face
as he searched his subject's eyes and, with a wave,
    invited him still closer.
The poet, now flushing deeply, walked the last few paces.
    "My lovely Catullus! A plume?
    You are deceived! Ah, Catullus!"
awarding with one hand a lingering caress
an inlaid Roman dagger with the other.

Smiling now again and eyeing his prey intently
    "Come, now, sweet Catullus. A last boon
    for your Emperor. Bleed for our noble friends
    and Caesar!"
Catullus shuddered, his face a deadly pallor.
The Emperor cajoled before the transfixed throng.
    "Now, now! For shame!" he pleaded, whinnied.
    "One small vein; a poet's vein for Caesar!"
The moment lengthened, the two in silent pantomime, and then
    "Please Caesar! Bleed!"
as the smile faded.

Invocation

The poet, strangely, was going blind
and, blind, he wore a coiling serpent on his head
the skull of the serpent flat, the length of the poet's head
the reptile's diamond head a crown on the bone of his skull
its sinuous length trailing down behind,
and thus, being blind, he could see.

But he lost his footing and fell
and the serpent writhed on the parquet floor.
And the poet struck it
and it reared, uncoiling its terrible length
and the fangs gleamed in a curving arc
and sank into the flesh,
but he had no fear of it
and again he struck it, and again
and we cried out, alarmed that he abuse the serpent
but again he struck and the diamond reared
    and flashed
and blood was on the polished floor.

The serpent coiled once more its terrible length
and climbing, remounted the poet's skull
nor was he afraid.

For a long time, we brooded on these things.

When I Die

From an old Negro spiritual

I wanta die easy when I die
Just pass on easy, Lord, when I die
Don't want no shoutin and no screamin
No kickin and no pleadin
I wanta die easy, Lord, when I die.

No reprimandin, please Lord
When I die
No what I should of done
Or could of done
Or, Lord, you know
If I'd been able
I surely would of done.
Just let me
      cross
           on
                over
My time to go is come
I wanta die easy, Lord, when I die.

Like a pigeon in the evening
Like a lamb come home at sunset
Like when Mary
   kissed her baby
I wanta die easy, Lord, when I die.

I Have Heard of a City

Upon a sloping path
   in shelves of streaming sun
I shall one day come home again
   the last course run.

Through perils that I had not known
   across an alien rock and clay
Upon a sudden turning there
   my laggard steps shall know the way.

Glimpsed faintly from a far off place
   beyond a harsh and unknown range
My feet shall find a near approach
   that is not strange.

On the last sloping path
   upon the arrows of the sun
I shall one day come home again
   and all is done.

145 Cliff Ave
Winthrop MA
02152
617) 846-1996